Original title: Verse in Vigor

Copyright © 2023 Swan Charm Publishing
All rights reserved.

Author: Daisy Dewi
Editor: Jessica Elisabeth Luik
ISBN 978-9916-39-478-6

Verse in Vigor

Daisy Dewi

Chants of Champions

Upon the fields of victory bright,
Our heroes stand in glory's light,
With every trial they have faced,
In triumph's arms they are embraced.

Their courage roars like thunder's call,
In unity they never fall,
For every foe that lies in wait,
Champions seal their rightful fate.

With medals hung and flags unfurled,
They stand as giants in the world,
Their stories echo through the years,
In chants that conquer all fears.

Lines of Lifeblood

Threads of life weave tapestries,
Intricate as ocean's breeze,
Each heartbeat writes a line of fate,
In the book of time, we can't negate.

Joy and sorrow in the blend,
Beginnings meet their eventual end,
Through the lines of life that twine,
We sip the bittersweet of time.

Bridges burn and new ones form,
In the face of every storm,
The lines of lifeblood, thin and strong,
Carry our restless hearts along.

Paeans to Power

In halls of might where echoes reign,
The powerful lift their proud refrain,
Paeans sung to the strength they wield,
Like towers on life's battlefield.

The will to conquer, to outlast,
To hold dominion, vast and vast,
In every word, the force imbued,
A testament to power accrued.

Narratives of mighty deeds,
They plant like everlasting seeds,
The peans rise and swell and tower,
As monuments to earthly power.

Syllables of Stone

Carved upon the mountain's face,
Enduring time, the stonemason's grace,
Syllables set in earth's own skin,
Speak of epochs deep within.

Granite words in silence tell,
Of ancient crypts and wishing well,
The verse of earth, so strong, so long,
Echoes in the stone's own song.

Monuments of the past arise,
Their stories reach to modern skies,
In syllables of stone, unthrown,
We read the history once unknown.

Villanelles of Vigor

With vibrant voice the vigor flows,
A dance of words in rhythmic throws,
The heart of life within it glows,
The spirit, ever upward goes.

In every line, a truth is sown,
Through metaphors the mind has known,
With every verse the light is shone,
A vigor through the verses grown.

Each stanza bursts with life anew,
The old departs, in comes the new,
A villanelle both firm and true,
Its vigor stands against the blue.

In ends the echo of the start,
The vigor beats within the heart,
The poet plays the crucial part,
In every end, a brand new start.

Brave Bard's Ballad

Upon the stage of ages vast,
The brave bard sings the future past,
With every note, a spell he casts,
The echoes of his voice will last.

His tales of heroes, dragons slain,
The maidens fair, the lover's pain,
Each ballad a unique refrain,
A tapestry of life's domain.

The strings of lyres pluck the night,
Under the canopy of twilight,
The bard's words flying like a kite,
Each verse a beacon burning bright.

Through every stanza, courage weaves,
Into the heart of one who believes,
The ballad breathes as audience heaves,
The brave bard's tale never deceives.

Indomitable Intonations

With voice that soars o'er mountain height,
The indomitable takes flight,
Each intonation a display of might,
A symphony of the day and night.

The resolute tones circle high,
Defiant of the earthly tie,
With every verse, they multiply,
The sound of will that will not die.

This anthem of the unyielded will,
Through storms and calm, it echoes still,
It rides the winds, it climbs the hill,
Each note a step, a triumphal drill.

Indomitable, the song prevails,
Against the gale that fiercely wails,
Through every chapter, the heart hails,
In intonations, the spirit sails.

Rhyme in Rally

Spectators cheer with might and main
Through dusty tracks carved upon the plain
Engines roar and tyres screech
In rhythm's embrace, the finish they breach

Each driver with eyes on the prize ahead
With every turn, excitement is fed
In unison, hearts with the engines rev
For victory's verse, to the limits they cleave

The checkerboard flag flutters in time
As the victor's anthem begins to chime
A symphony of success, a rhythmic feat
Where velocity and verse seamlessly meet

Conviction in Couplets

Stand firm in faith, with courage clad
In conviction's couplets, never sad

Resolve that runs through every word
Ensuring that every voice is heard

Step boldly forth, without retreat
With couplets crafted, none can defeat

In life's great book, your anthem scribed
In stanzas strong, your spirit imbibed

Iambic Invincibility

In measured meter, steps are made
With iambic feet, the lines parade
Each unstressed beat, followed by stress
Patterns that time cannot suppress

Heroes in stories, old and new
Their epic tales told with a meter true
Invincible rhythms frame each fight
In iambs that pulse from morn till night

Shakespearean plays with power imbued
By iambic charm are minds subdue'd
A sonnet's armor, strong and stable
Against fate's thrust, they remain able

Verve in Verses

With verve in verses, the poets write
Their quills, like swords in the muse's fight
Against silence, that blank, empty space
Their lines charge forth, a formidable lace

The stanza's strength, in each line it wields
Crosses the page, literary shields
With every rhyme, a blow is struck
Against indifference, their verses tuck

In the reader's heart, they plant their seed
With passionate verse to their cries they heed
A flourish here, a cadence there
In their poetic prowess, they freely share

Fervor in Form

Passion penned upon the page,
In fiery lines where feelings wage.
Each stanza strikes with lover's force,
The fervor's form, a poetic source.

Ebullient words within me burn,
Through every twist and tender turn.
Rhythms rise in heated dance,
Emotions play, and thoughts advance.

Muse's embrace stokes the fire,
Lines alight with burning desire.
Ink ignites, where passions swarm,
The poet's page forever warm.

Unyielding Utterances

Words, they wield an earnest edge,
Undaunted truths that time must pledge.
Steadfast speech in stormy seas,
Unyielding utterances never cease.

Voices venture, bold and brave,
In the caverns of the mind they cave.
Echoing eternity's unwavering call,
These phrases stand, they never fall.

In articulation's ardent hold,
Expressions dress in courage bold.
Syntax strong and grammar tight,
The power of prose to sway the night.

Metrical Muscle

With metrical muscle and rhythmic might,
The poet flexes, in verse takes flight.
Through syllables that sway and stress,
The power of the poem they do impress.

Metered lines craft mighty blows,
Form and structure aptly chose.
In the cadence, the strength does lie,
Building castles in the sky.

Stanzas strain with sculptured force,
Where language bends to chart its course.
The poem's punch, in tight constraint,
Displays the muscle words can paint.

Epic Echoes

In the hall of legends where echoes dance,
A tale is spun, a piercing lance.
Heroes of old with valorous stance,
Their epic saga, time's expanse.

Warriors bold in battle's trance,
Fought through the storm, the dark expanse.
With each fierce blow and glancing glance,
Their stories woven, fate's advance.

Dragons soared with fiery breath,
Scales agleam, eyes promising death.
Mighty roars shook the earth beneath,
Champions met their fiery teeth.

In whispers now the echoes play,
Of ancient times and warriors grey,
The pride and glory of their day,
Live on in hearts, forever stay.

Poems of Prowess

Upon the whispered winds of time,
A poet's prowess, words in line.
Each meter matched, each verse to rhyme,
A crafted jewel, pristine, sublime.

With pen in hand, I cast my spell,
Through stories told, in imagination dwell.
A prowess proving, powerful and swell,
In every stanza, my soul to quell.

Words, like warriors, march in tune,
Across the pages, their power immune.
Crafting visions beneath the moon,
Sharing whispers of a foregone dune.

Their strength in silence, rhythms bold,
A tapestry of tales untold.
In poems of prowess, hearts unfold,
In lines of art, life's essence is scrolled.

Cadenced Courage

With each cadence comes the drum,
The march of time, it does not succumb.
Bravery beats a rhythm, numb,
In the heart where courage comes from.

The footsteps fall on hallowed ground,
Cadenced courage in pulsing sound.
Each staccato step a battleground,
Where fear is lost and strength is found.

Arise, stand tall, the brave and true,
With beats that echo, bright and new.
In every measure, courage grew,
And to themselves, they remain due.

In the syncopated pause of war,
Lie tales of those who've gone before.
Their courage chants forevermore,
In the melody of legend's lore.

Haikus of Heartiness

Mountain's breath so bold,
Hearts of nature, strong, unfold.
Silent stories told.

Ocean's depth conceals,
Hearty spirits, water wheels.
Life's vast appeal.

Forest whispers wise,
Sturdy trunks reach to the skies.
Gentle strength belies.

Sun's hearty embrace,
Enlivens the world's vast space.
Kindness warms our race.

Lively Limericks

There once was a cat quite agile,
Who danced in a manner so fragile.
It leapt without care,
With such debonair flair,

The mouse watched on, somewhat hostile.
Its whiskers twitched to the beat,
As the cat tapped with its feet.
The mouse could not pretend,
It was charmed in the end,

The two danced off down the street.
In harmony with paws and tail,
Their jovial romp did not fail.
Whiskers and fur in the breeze,
They pranced with such ease.

Ballads of the Brave

Of heroes old and legends vast,
A tale of bravery unsurpassed.
With sword in hand, and shield so staunch,
They fought till dusk, from dawn to launch.

In valleys deep, on mountains high,
Their valor soared, touched the sky.
No beast too fierce, no odds too grave,
They stood their ground, forever brave.

Through storms they marched, in silent might,
Against the dark, they were the light.
Their armor gleamed, their spirits burned,
With every victory hard-earned.

Sinewy Sonnets

Upon a page, fresh words entwine,
To craft the strength of sonnet's spine.
Each line does flow with purpose keen,
In structured grace, a sight unseen.

With quill in hand, the poet's plea,
To capture life, in verse set free.
The form constrains, yet thoughts expand,
A sinewy dance, at heart's command.

The meter strict, with rhyme in place,
A story told with gentle grace.
The sonnet holds, within its frame,
Emotions wild, tamed but untamed.

Meter Made of Steel

With words of iron, rhymes of steel,
Poetic gears turn with zeal.
The stanzas march, in lined array,
The meter's might on full display.

Unyielding tempo, firm and strong,
A forge of phrases, crafted long.
Each verse a link in chainmail's song,
Resilient, robust, and lifelong.

In cadence strict, the poem's form,
The verses weather any storm.
Forged in fire and cooled in strife,
A metal meter, full of life.

Sturdy Stanzaic Stones

Upon the ground, these rocky forms,
Unmoved, they stand, in storms they're born.
Each grain of sand, a story old,
In sturdy stanzas, tales are told.

Unyielding to the winds of change,
In their clasp, time's secrets exchange.
The mountain's might, in each stone's stance,
Holds the weight of forgotten dance.

These stones recite the earth's deep rhymes,
Resilient through the harshest times.
Eroded not by rain nor rote,
In stanzaic strength, they stoically dote.

Lively Lexicon

A dance of diction in delight,
With every word, a world ignites.
A marriage of meaning and muse,
In the lexicon, life infuse.

Phrases pirouette on the page,
Lexical leaps, from stage to stage.
Vocabulary vast and vivid,
Linguistic leaps, lively, livid.

Syntax swings in seamless array,
Connotations contest and play.
In the lively lexicon's laugh,
Wisdom waltzes on readers' behalf.

Sonnets of Surge

In torrents of verses, truths converge,
Through metered lines, life's surge we urge.
Pentameter paints passion's plea,
In sonnets' swings, we set thoughts free.

A rush of rhyme, the heart's deep drum,
In every line, emotions come.
The surging sonnets, love's refrain,
Lift the soul beyond earthly plane.

With structured rhythms, beats align,
Our surging sonnets' sweet design.
In them, the spirit finds its form,
Through tempests' tales, we weather the storm.

Verses of Valor

With words as weapons, wielded wise,
Poetic soldiers strategize.
In verses, valor's voice resounds,
Upon the page, where courage bounds.

The stanzas march in metered tread,
Lines lay bare what's oft unsaid.
In rhymes, the ranks of valor rise,
In the ink, our honor lies.

Ballads of bravery and might,
In poems, we prepare the fight.
In the verses, valor weaves,
The tales of triumph no one grieves.

Sestinas of Solidarity

In unity, we find a common thread,
We weave a tapestry that's broad and deep,
Each stitch a pact that's silently conveyed,
A quilt of many colors, warmth to keep.

Together standing firm against the storm,
Our voices meld into a powerful hum,
In every heart a light begins to form,
Creating melodies that overcome.

With solidarity, our woes are halved,
A network of strong hands will share the weight,
Through every challenge, we remain unscathed,
Together we decide our common fate.

We march in sestinas of purpose bold,
Our chorus of support will never fold.

Dynamic Dactyls

Verses dance, a rhythmic, dynamic flow,
Each syllable a beat, a dactyl's stride,
With meter set, the words begin to glow,
In patterns, where the poet's thoughts abide.

The tempo lifts the spirit, soars high,
Creates a pulse that stirs the quiet air,
Emotion rides the current of the sky,
In dactyls' wings, it floats without a care.

Language leaps, like rivers that cascade,
Each drop a note within the grand parade,
Dynamic range of sound is now displayed,
In verses where the dance of words is made.

Dactylic steps, they twist and then unfold,
A story in the meter is retold.

Odes to Fortitude

O Fortitude, in storms you are the lighthouse,
The steadfast beacon guiding us through night,
Your solid rock, against the waves, does spite,
You give us strength to face the tempest's might.

Within the soul, a sturdy oak does grow,
With roots entwined in earth, you stand so proud,
Each leaf a testament to unbowed vow,
Odes sing of bravery that's not cowed.

When trials loom and daunting is the climb,
Your whispers in our hearts are like a drum,
Resounding with the beat of courage's chime,
Ensuring we're not fragile, nor succumb.

We pen our ode to steadfastness, our guide,
The essence of persistence amplified.

Robust Rhymes

In robust rhymes, our language shows its strength,
The verses flex as muscles made of words,
Each line a dumbbell lifted at its length,
A gymnasium where the mind's heard.

The poet is the coach that drives the verse,
Encouraging the stanza to be bold,
With metaphor and simile converse,
New tales of olden times are deftly told.

A sonnet's frame, the weights it does sustain,
In structured form, it showcases its might,
The quatrain's power, not a single strain,
A rhyme that lunges forward into light.

So let these rhymes robustly march ahead,
In rhythms that are learned, and loved, and spread.

Vibrant Versification

In every heart the colors lie,
Painting dreams that sail the sky.
Verses bloom as flowers wild,
Nature's own beloved child.

Words they dance in vibrant hue,
Stories old, and narratives new.
Symphony of sounds untamed,
In every stanza, life proclaimed.

Through the fabric of each line,
Emotions weave and souls entwine.
A canvas broad, a spectrum vast,
In vivid verse, the die is cast.

Echoing the heart's desire,
Innocent as morning's fire.
Poetry with its vibrant flair,
Whispers secrets into the air.

Trochaic Tenacity

Steady beats the trochaic drum,
Calling poets to come and hum.
Words in cadence, firm and clear,
Marching on, they persevere.

Eager hearts that never rest,
Giving voice to the unexpressed.
With tenacity they mold,
Tales in trochee, fiercely bold.

In the arena of the mind,
Rhythms strict, yet never confined.
Battle-hardened, they align,
Drawing strength from meter's spine.

Boldly standing up to time,
The trochees ring in simple chime.
With each measure, they endure,
In the dance of language, pure.

Poise in Poetry

In the whisper of the leaves,
Poetry weaves its silent sieves,
Catching moments light and fair,
With the poise of a dancer's air.

Letters align in quiet grace,
Across the page, they gently trace.
Each word, a soft and measured stride,
In the waltz of verses, they collide.

With tender touch upon the strings,
A symphony of musings brings.
A balance struck between two thoughts,
In the space where poise is taught.

Gently, the poet's hand does guide,
Where emotions and wisdom reside.
Offering reflections poised and pure,
In this art, hearts find their cure.

Profound Portraits in Poem

Words craft faces never seen,
In the poet's quiet dream.
Lines do sketch with care profound,
On the parchment's boundless ground.

Eyes that whisper hidden tales,
Lips that hold a thousand gales.
Each stroke brings a soul to life,
Canvas cut as though with knife.

With metaphor as their brush,
Poets paint in solemn hush.
Crafting images that stay,
Long after day fades to gray.

Portraits etched in verses deep,
In the reader's mind they seep.
Forever in poetic form,
Each face with verse, is thus reborn.

Echoes of Exuberance

Amidst the twilight's tender glow,
A symphony of joy we sow.
The stars above in dance convene,
To serenade the night unseen.

Two hearts entwined with fervent zest,
Their laughter spreads to all the rest.
A leap, a twirl, spirits ascend,
In exuberance that knows no end.

Nature's chorus joins the spree,
A cascade of pure reverie.
Waves of mirth that rise and surge,
In vibrant life, they merge and merge.

With every echo, soft and clear,
New memories hold dear and dear.
Time captures this in splendid hue,
The joy that birthed an evening new.

Alliterations of Ardor

With words woven whimsically wide,
Passionate pulses persistently preside.
An alluring allure, ably aligned,
Tenderly tracks the tides of the mind.

Boldly the breath of bravery breathes,
As ardent aspirations the soul achieves.
Grasping gambits, gamboling gay,
Hearts hail the hum of harmony's heyday.

Fierce feeling flits through flaxen fields,
Where ardor's anthem ardently yields.
In the interstice of intense intent,
Love's language lands its lasting accent.

Syllables strummed in seamless symmetry,
Frames the fervent furnace of fantasy.
Sowing seeds of spirited splendor,
Ardor's alliterations always tender.

Hymns of the Herculean

Upon brawny backs and solid shoulders,
Stands the legacy of ages' boulders.
With Herculean hymns that heave and hoist,
The titans' triumphs are forever voiced.

Unyielding in their unflagging strive,
Their echoes embolden the will to thrive.
The pounding power of potent pound,
Uphold the legends of lore profound.

The forge of fortitude flames fierce,
In the molten might that martyrs pierce.
With every heft and hardy haul,
The stoutest spirits refuse to fall.

Behold the behemoths' hallowed halls,
Where determination never stalls.
In every strain and stressful stretch,
Herculean heroes their heavens etch.

Measures of Mettle

In the cauldron of challenge, character is cast,
Measures of mettle are made to last.
It's not the trials, but how we respond,
That sculpts the steel of which we're fond.

Through tempests tossed and torrents tried,
The truest temper is not denied.
In the fire forged, amid adversity,
Resilience radiates with certainty.

Valor's vessel veers not from verity,
Honor-bound, it harbors no disparity.
Mettle's music is a marching muse,
Guiding the gallant, no path they refuse.

Stand steadfast, for strength stems from strife,
Mettle is measure and meaning of life.
With courage, we claim our narrative thread,
In the measures of mettle, our spirits are wed.

Allegories of Alacrity

Within the dawn's brisk, gentle sway,
Fleet as a deer that bounds away,
Alacrity, we clasp so tight,
Like morning's first and rosy light.

Swift through the fields of thought we roam,
In speed we find a transient home,
Quickening pulse and lively cheer,
Carry our souls far from here.

Eager heart beats with rapid fire,
Each moment filled with fresh desire,
The morrow's hopes on swift wings tread,
By zealous lively dreams we're led.

Our sprightly steps defy the night,
As stars twinkle back with delight,
In allegories softly cast,
We find our spirited repast.

Spirited Sonority

In whispered tones of evening's sigh,
The symphony of sky does lie,
Each note a breath, each breath a tone,
In sonorous beauty, fully grown.

The melody rides on the breeze,
Through rustling leaves and swaying trees,
It dances with a lively zest,
In the thrumming heart within our chest.

Now crescendo rises, bold and clear,
Nature's chorus for all to hear,
Singing aloud in unity,
Spirited sonority.

Hushed lullaby as night does fall,
The quiet after the bugle's call,
Still, in silence, sound does abide,
The echo of the day, our pride.

Heartfelt Hexameters

Upon the page in measured line,
The poet spills his heart's design,
In hexameters, he finds his muse,
Heartfelt words he cannot refuse.

Each line a rhythm, beats and flows,
A river of verse that ebbs and grows,
With every cadence, tender, true,
In ancient style, emotions brew.

The storied Greeks with epic tales,
Found in these meters, winds that wails,
So too, our modern voice intones,
With heartfelt hexameters, love enthrones.

In six-footed beats, we confide,
Our deepest joys and fears inside,
Lyrical dance of old and new,
In each line, a world to view.

Audacious Aubades

Crimson streaks adorn the sky,
Day's young light begins to spy,
Upon the whispers of the night,
Audacious aubade takes its flight.

Songbirds echo the daybreak's call,
Their melodies climb and fall,
In gentle hymns of early light,
They serenade the fleeing night.

Lovers part with a tender kiss,
Clutching the moments of night's bliss,
With each strain of dawn's early song,
They'll remember night long gone.

Awakening world takes its stage,
The sun ascends, day turns its page,
In this song of dawn's new embrace,
Life's earnest passions we ever chase.

Ballads of the Brave

In whispered tales of ancient days,
With swords that cleave and shields that blaze,
The brave stood firm against the wave,
Their steadfast hearts the kingdom save.

Upon the craggy mountain side,
Where eagles in the aether glide,
The heroes fought with valor true,
Their crimson banners bold it flew.

The clashing steel, the battle's roar,
The victory march of those of yore,
They left their legend on the field,
With iron wills, they'd never yield.

Through stormy night and arrow's rain,
The brave may fall, yet rise again,
Their sagas sung beneath the stars,
In ballads penned from noble scars.

Elegies of Endurance

When shadows fall and lights grow dim,
And hopes recede on horizon's rim,
The souls that bear life's heavy load,
Carve paths of endurance they've bestowed.

Through silent struggles, they persevere,
In hidden battles, shed unseen tear,
Yet every dawn, they rise anew,
With strength to face the morning's dew.

Their silent stories echo deep,
Whispers of promises they keep,
A testament to the unseen fight,
A torch that burns through the darkest night.

An ode to those who quietly brave,
Storms of life, and fortunes grave,
In endurance, find a subtle grace,
With stoic peace upon their face.

Cadence of Courage

Listen close to the beating drum,
That calls the courageous to overcome,
The steady rhythm within their chest,
Guides them through each daunting quest.

Against the tempest, they take their stand,
An unyielding force, a resolute band,
In the cadence of courage, they find their tune,
Under the glow of the silver moon.

With each bold step upon the stone,
Through paths untamed and lands unknown,
Their spirit's beat, a fearless song,
Composing a history, proud and long.

For every challenge that they face,
They march ahead with measured pace,
In every heart, the drumming roars,
In cadence sweet, the brave soul soars.

Quatrains of Quintessence

In essence pure, the soul's bright fire,
A spark that dances, never to tire,
Quatrains capture this fleeting glimpse,
Of the quintessence within, that never dims.

Each verse a vessel for timeless truth,
A beacon for the elders and the youth,
In words that flow like a gentle stream,
They paint the picture of a dreamer's dream.

In the quiet still of reflection deep,
These quatrains in the heart shall keep,
A mirrored pool of our inner light,
Revealing thoughts that take their flight.

Upon the page, a dance, a weave,
A tapestry that minds conceive,
The quintessence of life, in quatrains told,
In poetry's embrace, it turns to gold.

Paeans of Potency

Mighty mountains rise with grace,
Solid strength in earth's embrace.
Jagged giants touch the skies,
In potent poise, nature's guise.

Stone and sinew, break nor bend,
Enduring power shall never end.
Rivers carve with potent flow,
Molding lands with steady blow.

Iron will and steadfast might,
In every dawn, through every night.
No falter in the force we find,
A paean of the potent kind.

Force of arms and strength of mind,
Untamed potency, not confined.
In every pulse, the power thrives,
Through potent paeans, vigor survives.

Verses of Valiance

Brave the battle, face the fray,
Valiant hearts lead the way.
Coursing courage through the vein,
In valorous verse, heroes reign.

Sword and shield in hand they take,
For honor's sake, the risks they stake.
With dauntless deeds that speak so loud,
In valor's verses, we stand proud.

Unyielding under siege and storm,
Noble spirits will transform.
Facing fears with chests out-thrown,
Valiance in each verse is sown.

The gallant charge, the stalwart stand,
Withstands the trial, time's demand.
Their tales told in daring dance,
In verses of valiance, our spirits enhance.

Harmonics of Heart

Soft whispers of the lover's lute,
Tender touch, the heart's soft flute.
In harmonics sweet and clear,
Speak of love that we hold dear.

Beats in sync, an echoed sound,
In our chests, where love is found.
Melodic pulse, together bound,
In harmonics of heart, our lives are wound.

Loving gently, healing art,
In each rhythm, a new start.
Serenading souls to chart,
A world where harmonics of heart impart.

Soothing strains that sway and part,
In unity, a work of art.
Listen close, the heart won't lie,
Harmonics sing as life goes by.

Dithyrambs of Drive

As fiery steeds with untamed mane,
So is the sprit we can't restrain.
With dithyrambs of drive, they race,
A burning zeal that we embrace.

Our goals ahead, these passions surge,
Compelling urge that we must purge.
With each stride, we're more alive,
In driving dithyrambs, we thrive.

Forge ahead, no rest nor slumber,
In our hearts, the burning cumber.
With every toil, effort rife,
We sculpt our fate, we carve our life.

Ambition's torch, held up so high,
Its flames lick at the endless sky.
Driven by this inner dive,
In dithyrambs of drive, we arrive.

Epic of Energy

In the heart of the sun, a fiery blaze,
Fusion's alchemy sets the sky ablaze.
Unseen power swirling in the stratosphere,
The cradle of life, the source so clear.

Rivers that run with a force untamed,
The wind's wild dance, never to be claimed.
Mountains that hold the ancient sun's glow,
Nature's pure strength in every snow.

Atoms entwined in a cosmic twist,
Electric currents in the mist.
From the crack of dawn to the evening's yawn,
The pulse of the world carries on.

Majestic turbines, spin and hum,
Harvesting breezes that come.
In the epic of energy, bold and grand,
Lies the power of an unseen hand.

Savvy Sijo

Wisdom distilled in lines so sleek,
Verses that harbor the answers we seek.
A sage's journey through patterns of thought,
Ingenious Sijo, with insight fraught.

Each syllable carved like a jewel so fine,
Clear-cut and shining in each disciplined line.
Order and chaos in tight interlace,
In the space of the poem, time and place.

Culture's breath captured in rhythmic flow,
Narratives penned with an ancient glow.
Savvy Sijo speaks through the ages,
Profound simplicity on history's pages.

Zealous Zapfendels

Oh, the Zapfendels, creatures of zeal,
In the enchanted forest, they spin and reel.
With fantastical frolics and leaps so high,
The forest awakens, the spirits fly.

From the twilight canopy to the mushroom rings,
Their laughter echoes as the night bird sings.
They dance 'neath the stars, so bright and so tender,
In a world untouched, pure and splendor.

Flickering shadows amidst the trees,
A ballet of leaves in the autumn breeze.
Zealous Zapfendels, with joy unbound,
Sprinkling magic all around.

When the morning breaks, they vanish from sight,
Leaving the woods in a tranquil delight.
Yearning for evening's playful spells,
To frolic again, the Zealous Zapfendels.

Titular Triumph

In a name, essence is captured and bound,
Echoes of history in syllables found.
Majesty dwells in the titles we bear,
Each a story, a triumph to share.

On pages of legend, the characters bold,
In scripts of silver and ink made of gold.
The weight of a crown in a single phrase,
In the title, the saga of heroes ablaze.

With letters and words, we claim our space,
Our deeds and our dreams leaving their trace.
In the firmament of time, names engraved,
Titular triumphs, forever saved.

Glory recounted in monuments high,
Legacies whispered 'neath the vast sky.
In the name we carry, our fates are spun,
For in the title, the victory is won.

Bold Ballads

Champions ride through thunderous tales,
Their armors glint as daylight pales.
Quests of valor where the brave prevail,
Songs of glory that forever regale.

In the hall of echoes, their stories enthrall,
Each verse a memory, legends stand tall.
Fear not the darkness nor the gallows call,
For in bold ballads, heroes never fall.

With every stanza, courage takes flight,
A symphony of wills burning ever so bright.
Against roaring winds and the blackest night,
Their anthem resounds, a beacon of light.

To live in hearts we leave behind,
Is never to die, in these ballads enshrined.
Bold in spirit, unyielding in mind,
The balladeer's voice, through ages aligned.

Potent Paean

Sing a potent paean for the earnest earth,
For rolling seas and the soil's worth.
Melodies deep as the roots of trees,
Ballads that drift on the summer breeze.

Praise to the sun-swept, bounteous fields,
To the bounty that nature's garden yields.
Warbling notes that in hearts are sealed,
Harmonies in the harvest's golden shields.

A chorus rises for the mountains high,
Their peaks aglow 'neath the morning sky.
The streams below hum a soft reply,
In this paean where tranquility lies.

Resound, resound, o voices clear,
In adoration of all we hold dear.
Potent paean that the earth shall hear,
An enduring hymn across all spheres.

Anthems of Ardor

In the fire of youth, anthems rise,
A burning cadence in fervent eyes.
Passion's verse on the wind it flies,
Sung by hearts that won't compromise.

Roar the refrains of ardent dreams,
Where every pulse with yearning teems.
Echoing where the rosy dawn gleams,
Anthems spring from audacious streams.

Love's own voice in a fervid tone,
An undying echo from the cornerstone.
Where ardor's seeds are generously sown,
In these anthems, desire is grown.

The tapestry of fervor weaves,
As every stanza fervently breathes.
In the chorus, the spirit achieves,
Ardor pledged that never deceives.

Pulsing Poetics

Strike the cords of the pulsing poetic heart,
Infusing life where the blank pages start.
In every line, a beat, a living part,
Stanzas throb with the artist's smart.

Cadenced heartbeats in ink do spill,
Verses flow, the poet's quill to thrill.
With each rhyme, a surge, a quivering frill,
Poetry's pulse does the canvas fill.

Metrical throbs in a rhythmic strain,
Echoing the poet's joy and pain.
Pulsed in pleasure, pulsed in disdain,
Poetics written in the heart's domain.

With every pulse, the words align,
Symphony of verse in sync and design.
Emotions dance, sentiments entwine,
In the pulsing poetics of the line.

Grit in Ghazals

With every verse, a story's breath, the struggle boldly sown,
Perseverance weaves its thread through every line that's grown.
Challenge faced at break of dawn, under the crescent moon,
In every couplet, grit unfurls, a strength that's rarely shown.

Through winding roads and steeped in hope, the poet's voice takes flight,
Echoes of battles fought within, from darkness into light.
Tales of endurance etched in ink upon the aging page,
Each stanza stands, a testament, against life's raging fight.

The Ghazal sings of trials faced, the heartaches we reclaim,
A soothing balm upon the soul, adversity to tame.
Melodies of courage rise, in harmonies, they heal,
The grit and grace intertwined, a timeless, fierce refrain.

Triumph in Tercets

In life's great play, a tercet's power can boldly hold the stage,
With just three lines of victory's voice, the mind it can engage.
A triad of emotion flows, and triumph it declares.

The trials of our yesteryears, in tercet form now caged,
Each line a step on victory's stair, as destiny is waged.
The past is but a stepping stone to future's brighter wares.

And so with pen in hand I craft a trio of success,
A celebration scribed in ink for all that we possess.
In tercets strong, our spirits soar, to bright horizons press.

Gallant Ghazals

In gallant ghazals, honor's vesture clothes each vibrant verse,
The noble acts, the valiant thoughts, through poets' lines disperse.
The majesty of courage found within the heart of man,
As couplets call to us to rise, their gallantry we rehearse.

For in these words, a chivalry that's stood the test of time,
Through every era, every age, in every land and clime.
We read of knights and heroes past, their deeds become our own,
The ghazals sing of legacies that never seem to wane.

The metered lines hold stories of the brave who've come before,
The gallant souls immortalized in poetic folklore.
Their strength depicted in each verse, a guiding light unfurled,
These gallant ghazals speak of valor, now and evermore.

Couplet Crusades

Upon the battlefield of verse, the couplet's might does rise,
A crusade waged with words so sharp, beneath the literary skies.
A pair of lines stands side by side, in solidarity,
Their rhythmic charge across the page, where truth meets fantasy.

For every rhyme a weapon used, to conquer doubt and fear,
These couplets march in metered time, their message loud and clear.
A quest for beauty, wisdom's light, in pairs they forge ahead,
To claim the hearts of readers with each turn of phrase that's led.

These couplet crusades carve the path for poets to inspire,
Through duets of emblazoned words, they kindle passion's fire.
The art of brevity in pairs, their strength we can't evade,
In every couplet's compact might, the essence is conveyed.

Free Verse of the Fierce

In the den where shadows box with light,
I stand with fists clenched, ready for the fight.
My spirit, unchained, roars like the surf,
Wild and fierce, I claim my own worth.

Where the brave dare to tread, I make my path,
Defiant, unyielding, to confront the wrath.
Through raging storms and whispers of doubt,
I rise, a fierce force, with a warrior's shout.

In every breath, a tempest brews,
Each heartbeat an anthem, courage infuses.
I weave strength from the loom of despair,
Fierce in resolve, none can compare.

I am the fire that warms the cold truth,
The relentless seeker of the fountain of youth.
In verses fierce, my story is told,
Unbridled, untamed, unapologetically bold.

Ghazals of Gumption

With gumption, I tread through days and nights unfurled,
In this labyrinth of life, my resolve is pearled.
Though challenges loom like mountains vast,
With a heart of grit, I shall hold fast.

Each dawn brings trials, new grounds to chart,
The map of ambition etched in my heart.
Courage, my compass, in the seas of strife,
Steering with gumption, I navigate life.

In the garden of dreams, where hope flowers bloom,
Through gumption, I ward off impending gloom.
My endeavors—seeds sown with determination,
Unfolding in hues of triumph's celebration.

With verses of vigor, the ink still wet,
My ghazals of gumption, in stone, are set.
A testament to the spirit, ever so plump,
Resilience penned in this poetic clump.

Sestinas of the Steadfast

Steadfast, like a beacon in the tempest's howl,
I stand unshaken by the waves that growl.
Endurance is the cloak that I don, so grand,
With fortitude woven by an artisan's hand.

Upon the anvil of time, my will is forged,
Against the hammering doubts, fiercely purged.
In the steadfast forge, my spirit's glow,
A sestina of steel, in twilight's show.

Loyal to dreams with unwavering sight,
I plant my flag upon the highest height.
The steadfast song, a ballad, long and sweet,
Scribed in the stars, a cosmic feat complete.

In every sestina's intricate design,
Is the steadfast heart's unbreakable line.
Through each verse it threads, a resilient seam,
Steadfast and true, the weaver's ultimate dream.

Limericks of Liveliness

There once was a spirit so sprightly,
Whose step in the dance was so lightly.
With a twirl and a tap,
No mishap or gap,
They moved through the room so brightly.

In a village where laughter rang true,
Limericks of liveliness grew.
With rhythms so witty,
And verses so pretty,
Joy in the heart justly ensued.

A jovial fellow of cheer,
Face beaming throughout the whole year.
With a laugh so hearty,
The life of the party,
His merriment always near.

A tale in each limerick lies,
Of happiness under the skies.
Where joy's never less,
With each rhyme we confess,
Liveliness wins the grand prize.

Forceful Free-Verse

Unbound by meter's rigid reins,
Adrift in liberty's vast sea,
Lines cascade like unchained rains,
Words wield their wild potency.

Each verse a torrent unrestrained,
A force where thoughts can roam and be,
No stanza neatly preordained,
Free-verse, the soul of poetry.

Breaking from tradition's tight grasp,
Concepts rise, then swell, then clasp,
Reveling in freedom's bold gasp,
Innovation in each breath's rasp.

Flow, the ink of human spirit,
Defy, the norms that would impair it,
Charge on, for you shall never fear it,
Create, with force in every merit.

Intrepid Idylls

In dales where golden sunlights stream,
Where adventure calls in whispers,
Brave souls tread where dreamers dream,
Their path lit with hope's bright flickers.

Beyond the tranquil, verdant fields,
Past the brook's soft, melodious laughs,
To daring heights where eagles yield,
The intrepid find their epigraphs.

Upon the mountain's craggy face,
Against the sky's embracing blue,
There lie tales no time can erase,
Of bold hearts staunch, and ever true.

In idylls where courage resides,
In brave pursuits that time betides,
Find spirits that adventure guides,
Intrepid lives that joy confides.

Force of Phrases

Assemble the legions of lexicons vast,
March forth with phrases aligned in contrast,
Lay siege to the silence with grammar amassed,
In the battle of wits, only words will outlast.

Flanks of metaphors, strong and diverse,
Cavalry of puns in the universe,
Infantry of syntax, for better or worse,
Wielding connotations as their curse.

Artillery of adjectives, loud and clear,
Bombarding the senses, far and near,
Similes striking like a spear,
A symphony of linguistics to hear.

In the end, when the prose has ceased,
And the quietude of peace released,
The force of phrases, never deceased,
Lives on in minds, forever increased.

Muscular Metaphors

Pumping iron in a gym of thought,
Biceps of imagery flex and flaunt,
Rippling through the mind, uncaught,
Muscular metaphors bear the brunt.

Lifting the weight of wisdom's wealth,
Deadlifting concepts for mental health,
Building endurance in stealth,
Powerlifting to express oneself.

With every rep, a new idea forms,
Sweat dripping like sentence storms,
Vivid visions breaking norms,
Narratives swell as emotion transforms.

Chiseled phrases in verbal sprees,
Squatting under heavy themes with ease,
Strength of language that none seizes,
As metaphors flex linguistic expertise.

Empowered Elegies

Steady beats the heart that knows its time,
To dance through shadows and embrace the climb.
Evening's sorrows, by morning, concede,
To the mighty dawn, with newfound creed.

Strength carves its script in whispers of night,
In every lost soul, reignites a light.
Past tears now seeds in life's vast garden,
Bloom into hope, burdens unburden.

Every elegy wears an armor of sorts,
In the silent resolve of the spirit's retorts.
Rising from whispers to empowered roars,
Charting a course to unopened doors.

The final verse, a triumphant decree,
Of a soul set free, daring to be.
Scribed in the skies, an endless plea,
In empowered elegies, we find the key.

Quatrains of Quiddity

In the essence of existence, insights gleam,
A quiddity found in the heart of a dream.
Mirrored truths in the depth of a glance,
Whispered life stories in a mystical dance.

Pondering the core, so delicate, so vast,
Quatrains capture the essence that will last.
Pulses of wisdom in syllables confined,
In four-lined verses, our truths intertwined.

Quiddity questions in the ink that flows,
Irrevocable answers that nobody knows.
Each stroke of the pen, a philosophy's seed,
Maturing into quatrains that souls heed.

In the beauty of brevity, meanings align,
Invisible threads that fatefully entwine.
Quatrains of quiddity, in simplicity dressed,
Reveal the profound, in their humble quest.

Verses Vigilant

With vigilant verses that watch over night,
Guarding the dreams until morning's light.
The guardians of thought, in rhythm they stand,
Shielding the silent, with a pen in hand.

Eyes open wide when the world is asleep,
Whispering wisdom secrets to keep.
In the stillness, the vigilant does find,
A muse that dances, an idea unconfined.

The vigilant heart, through darkness, it sees,
In each shadow, decoding life's mysteries.
With each stanza, a vigilant creed,
To stay awake while the world is in need.

In the final watch, before light reclaims,
Verses vigilant speak forgotten names.
The unsung heroes in history's weave,
In verses they breathe, in verses believe.

Rhymes Reinforced

In the fortress of language, rhymes reinforced,
Echoing power, with every word endorsed.
Intrepid expressions in rhythmical chain,
Joining together, an indomitable train.

Walls of conviction, built verse by verse,
Rhymes as the bricks, both blessing and curse.
A solid resolve that nothing can pierce,
In reinforced rhymes, the innermost fears disperse.

Stalwart they stand in the face of doubt,
A battalion of ballads, a lyrical shout.
Reinforcing belief, when uncertainty dawns,
Through the strength of a rhyme, new hope is drawn.

Steel-laced stanzas, resilient and sure,
In the cadence of courage, hearts endure.
The might of a metaphor, firm and composed,
In rhymes reinforced, true strength is exposed.

Whispers of Strength

In silence bloom resilient dreams,
Whispers of strength, soft yet supreme.
Gentle in form, yet fierce in fight,
Shadows unfold into the night.

Within the quiet, courage stirs,
Audible only to believers.
Murmurs that swell to a roar,
Building a fortress from the floor.

Echoes of power softly spoken,
Unseen threads of fate woven.
Standing firm when troubles throng,
Whispers of strength, a silent song.

Tales of valor softly tread,
In hushed tones, our fears we shed.
Strength in stillness, we conceal,
In whispers, truth is revealed.

Melody of Might

A reverberating, righteous sound,
Melody of might, where hope is found.
Strains of victory rise and swell,
Overcoming fears, breaking the spell.

Bass and treble in symphony,
Forge the anthem of the free.
Crescendoing in a mighty choir,
Music fuels the warrior's fire.

Notes that dance on wings of dawn,
Singing strength to carry on.
In every pitch, a sword is drawn,
Melody of might sings on and on.

Harmonies that can inspire,
Kindle courage, lift us higher.
Might in music, cadence strong,
In every note, we find our song.

Lyricism Unleashed

Unleashed are words that wield the truth,
Crafting visions of eternal youth.
Bold ideas cloaked in rhyme,
Marching forth through sands of time.

Mind's eye opens to the sun,
Lyricism, a revolution begun.
Stanzas of a world remade,
In verses bold, we wield the blade.

Poetic power in every line,
A lexicon of the divine.
Vivid imagery set to flight,
In the heart of day or cloak of night.

A torrent of verbiage floods our feasts,
Metaphors are now our beasts.
Words break free, the mind's release,
In lyricism we find our peace.

Stanzas of Stamina

Enduring lines that long withstand,
Poetry's power at your command.
Stanzas strong and full of life,
Conquering struggles, surviving strife.

Metered verse that paces breath,
Through each line, we cheat death.
Speaking stamina into souls,
Resolute rhymes that make us whole.

Each quatrain a step, a steady climb,
Verses marking beats of time.
In relentless rhythm, we advance,
Strength recited in a rhythmic dance.

Poems as pillars, steadfast, grand,
Support us when we can barely stand.
Stamina spoken in structured form,
Through stanzas fierce, we weather the storm.

Beacons in Blank Verse

Upon the silent seas of fate so vast,
In darkness deep where lost ambitions cast,
There shine the beacons bright of hope's firm mast,
Guiding through night's despair, the gales they outlast.

Each lighthouse stands, a sentinel of dreams,
Its light cuts through the shadowed, moonlit streams.
Unmoved by tempest's scream or tidal schemes,
It promises safe harbor in night's extremes.

For every soul afloat on life's wide brine,
Where stars above in distant heavens align,
Those beacons call across the brackish brine,
Offering their glow, a universal sign.

So may we steer by these fixed points of light,
Through currents unknown, out of the dark night,
Towards havens warm, towards the morning bright,
Where faith in dawn's approach defeats the fright.

Luminous Lyric

Glowing phrases twirl in melodious flight,
Notes on night air, painting silence bright,
The stars wink back as stanzas dance in sight,
A symphony of words in ardent height.

Harmonies spun from strands of soft moonbeam,
Rhythm in whispers, like a distant dream.
Each line a pulse within a silver stream,
Carried through the sky, a lyrical theme.

Verse draped in velvet, in the evening's arms,
Crooned beneath the heavens' charmed alarms.
An ode to night's seductive, quiet charms,
Wrapped in rhyme, the universe it warms.

In this luminous lyric, find escape,
From day's relentless, raucous soundscape.
Here, in quietude, the mind reshapes,
As tranquility in verse takes its shape.

Assertive Alliterations

Boldly bound, the brazen bells do toll,
Tales of temerity truly told.
Mighty murmurs move, making minds whole,
An audacious act, admirably bold.

Daring deeds, duly done during dawn,
Vivid visions vanquishing the yawning yawn.
Gallant gestures giving greatness spawn,
Fierce fantasies from the fathoms are drawn.

Tireless tides traverse the tempest's test,
Waves weaving warily to west and east.
Steady strides surge, seeking summit's crest,
Onward, outward, our opus not ceased.

Courage carries, conquers coming clouds,
Eager energies echo, ever loud.
Swiftly sailing, soars the spirit proud,
Alliterative anthem, avowed.

Unshakable Odes

Odes to the unyielding, unshaken by strife,
Foundations firm, in the quakes of life.
Steadfast and sure, like the edge of a knife,
Carving a path through hardship and rife.

Unshaken, unmoved by the gale's fierce breath,
Poetry praises the bold, dares death.
Verses of valor, eternal as earth,
Immortal lines of undying mirth.

Here's to the towers that teeter not,
To the unassailable courage sought.
In stanzas strong, the battles fought,
Are hymns of heroes, ne'er forgot.

In unshakable odes, the heart finds hold,
Golden stories in the annals of old.
The ink flows on, it's never too cold,
For tales of the fearless to be retold.

Rhythms of the Robust

In the thrumming heart of the awakened earth,
Echoes of the mighty, they find their birth.
Robust in spirit, in strength they trust,
Nature's deep cadence, the truest of just.

Upon the anvil, their will is wrought,
In the burning forges, life's battles fought.
With each resounding, persistent beat,
The robust rhythm never admits defeat.

Their voices carry through mountain and mist,
Where steel and bone and will insist.
In the orchestra of the enduring and vast,
The rhythms of the robust forever last.

And when the sun sinks, shadows embrace,
Even in darkness, their pulses race.
Time may weather, winds may gust,
But stand they will, the rhythms of the robust.

Lyrics of the Lionheart

With courage fierce, the lion's mane,
He roars his verse, bold and unchained.
A ballad of bravery, in his heart it starts,
A thunderous symphony in the lyrics of the lionheart.

In savannahs wide, under the sun's reign,
He faces each dawn, without fear or feign.
The pride's anthem in unity imparts,
The strength weaved within the lionheart's arts.

Across the land, his ballad rings clear,
The pride marches forth, without doubt or fear.
In every growl, in every furtive dart,
Resides the fierce love in the lion's heart.

A serenade to the wild, where his rule charts,
In every whisper of wind, in nature's ramparts.
With courage that kindles the night's dark, apart,
Forever echo the lyrics of the lionheart.

Cantos of Conviction

Upon the pages of the ageless stone,
The cantos of conviction are solemnly intoned.
Words etched with the power to inspire,
A hymn of resolve, an unwavering choir.

Mounting the pulpit in the soul's domain,
Each verse a testament, each refrain a claim.
With every measure, they the heart enrich,
Cantos resounding, never to glitch.

They speak of trials, of tribulations faced,
Of the staunch and steady, never disgraced.
In the echoing chamber of the bold and strict,
Sound the cantos of conviction, infinitely depict.

For when the wick of will burns low and affliction,
Is the time to chant aloud the cantos of conviction.
They lift us up, from the mire, they evict,
The voice of inner strength, forever predict.

Epics of the Energetic

In the realm of action, the bold take flight,
Their stories written in blazes of light.
Boundless vigor in their saga is etched,
In the epics of the energetic, their zest is sketched.

They dart and dance across life's grand stage,
In every movement, their spirit engage.
Vivid in their journey, they never rest,
For in the epics of the energetic, they're the quest.

As rivers flow with a relentless force,
So too do the energetic set their course.
With a gale of gusto, they face every test,
The heroes of haste, in fervor dressed.

In the sweep of time, their tale unfurls,
A whirlwind narrative that twists and twirls.
Always ahead, reaching for the apogee's crest,
In the epics of the energetic, they're forever blessed.

Printed in the USA
CPSIA information can be obtained
at www.ICGtesting.com
LVHW010028011223
765304LV00058B/678

9 789916 394786